OUR HUMAN RACE

44 POEMS FROM MY HEART TO YOURS

DESI TAHIRAJ

personal, or other damages.

CREATE

One day from my heart to my head a poem rose, pushed, provoked my thoughts and emotions that I could not stop repeating, repeating until pushed me to write in the middle of the night!

The next day another poem like a song went through my being! "No," I tried to stop myself. "You are not a poet! How are you going to share your deepest feelings? Writing poetry requires me to be open and be honest about my feelings."

That voice stopped as the passion won and went through pen and paper, which is the first step to truly expressing myself. The innermost thoughts allowed me to find true esteem!

Suddenly through words I felt the sound and music inside me.

I know that my mission is to heal the wounds of people in need and transform from the inside out. To reach the heart of people and bring love, prosperity; that we all care.

Throughout my life I appreciate the world and people around me. My family, friends and community are everything to me.

I strive to bring out the beauty in all of us, enhance ourselves so we will all be a better human race.

Desi Tahiraj

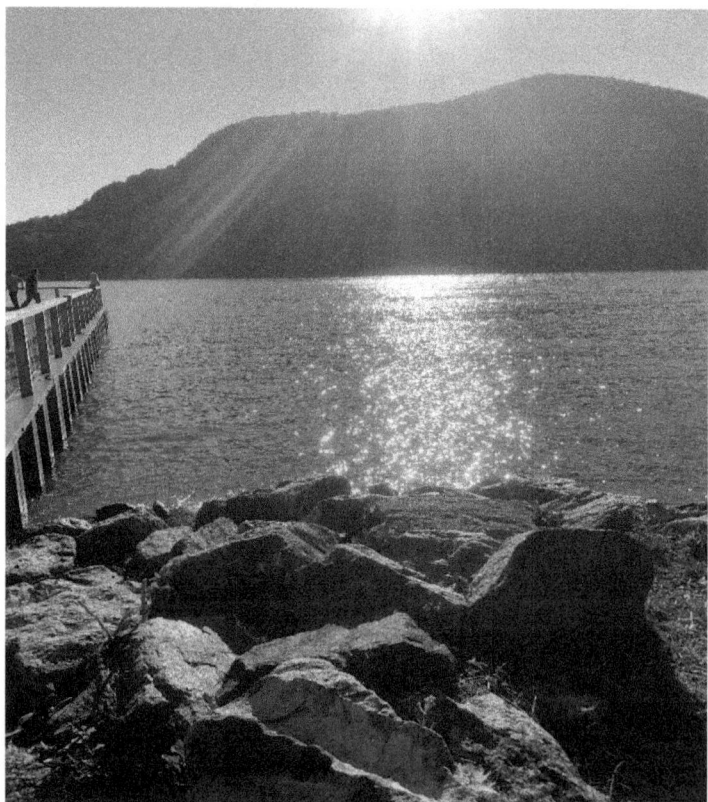

OUR HUMAN RACE

To our human race; a celebration for life!

This is a very special collection of writings. One part It's a celebration and a Call for all of us to wake up our purpose for unity that is the duty of humanity. One part love letter for people who are deeply, joyously in love - and who would love to have a way to express those deep and lasting feelings. Emotion's people feel but can't explain!

Once in a great while, and when it's least expected, a special miracle manages to find its way into two lucky people's lives. In a meant-to-be moment - the shared smiles, and the growing amazement that this closeness is beautifully real- comes to recognition that this is "it", the truly wonderful love of your life.

This book is a celebration of the humankind, building relationships that last forever. It is a gift that God gifted us, and it is our duty to raise our best qualities, our hopes and dreams that we all thrive with blessing to watch smiling faces everywhere.

SUCH AS WE ARE MADE OF, SUCH WE BE.
(Bible)

PART I

TOGETHER WE THRIVE!

Twenty years from now, you will be more disappointed by the things that you didn't do than by the ones you did do. So, throw off the bowlines. Sail away from the safe harbor. Catch the trade winds in your sails. Explore. Dream. Discover.

– Mark Twain –

Our Human Race

To be or not to be Shakespeare said one day,

Who knows what he experienced to come to that end!

Every one of us comes to one day realize

What is the truth that drives our life!

How heavenly is it that God gifted every one of us?

with talent that drives our life!

I am gifted with patience, purpose, determination, and drive

Solutions to find, the zest of love,

A student forever to serve the Divine!

What is your gift, dear one?

Tell us so we all share our gifts to our Divine!

Together we thrive no matter what

To build a better world for generations to come!

To show the Universe that we come to this world

to fulfill our duty of a good human on earth!

To learn not to be pitied, compassionate embrace

So, we enhance the greatness of the human's race!

To build a foundation that lasts forever like

Moses, Jesus, Socrates, who live forever!

We feed the good, not the bad and ugly

to rebuild and heal all wounded souls!

It's our duty on this day of our world!

To be or not to be Shakespeare said one day,

So, we all choose to be a great human race!

YOU AND ME!

It's funny how easily we judge others,

Funny when we can't see ourselves,

and funnier when we prejudice others

as we think "we are better than them!"

It's funny how often we fool ourselves

and it gets the better of us,

We can't see the beauty in others

as we are so busy within us!

We feel fear to speak our mind

to face our internal bias

to fight that urge of the apparent mind!

And be a better version of what we already are.

How we can't see

 that beauty lies in the eye of the beholder!

We cannot help but glare

at something that our physique can't accept.

What is diverse? It is not my kind!

Imagine if the other side thinks the same!

Our society would break down and our culture would be drained.

Assumptions are awful, ask a question instead

As clarity brings prosperity.

We are all able and fully capable

of crafting and building a great society.

WAKE UP!

Day in and day out

We tend to die inside out

We cannot see how great we are

And probably tend to not go far!

And as we grow and see one day

Our life is gone, and we ask how!

Dear one, wake up,

Shake up your past

Rise up your inner love!

Life as you see is a short trip

Make it as best as it could be.

Our life matters

In all senses

Live, sing LOVE

That's ALL that matters.

THE THEATER OF LIFE

Still breathe aloud – and the air vibrated
like acoustics that need to hear

the cathedral of Jesus

the cathedral raises me to remember

my desire which is screaming to come out

to live and live so trustfully, so singly,

servant, clean and disciplined.

Below under

full of candles standing on the floor, and
my desire!

There was so much of the world that I had
to chase,

to pack, set off to leave, vanish without a
trace.

Oh no I don't want to leave

a bit of anger and great expectation,
dedication.

I have always done what I was told.

In drops of rain, in the thorns of roses

the theater of life opens.

By the sun, at night in the deep blue sky

I grew so mindlessly overjoyed everywhere

In hallways, coffee shops revolving by themselves

There was too much to love,

and now there isn't worry.

Ah, wait till a warm hurricane comes with fumes ...

the reality without mercy!

Along with the line and through it ... no tears

So dry, so breathless,

quiet and pure as a peach it's everywhere.

A cry of pain that could have gotten loud and worse but not

beneath my breath, I hear,

no, baby you are not falling ... the sensation of falling off

Turned into fire, storm

Were night and slush and cold,

sleep on a sofa beside the door.

My hands laying under the lamp at shadowy gray knees

I knew nothing, nothing, nothing.

How did I come to be here?

I CRY

He stopped there and watching in despair

His flawless screaming as much as he can

Oh, my dear how you could not see

How bad is for you and me

Your anger, behavior got to change

Is well possible that you could change.

Oh no I can't change

I am too old to care

It's me and that's way it will be

My anger is good, so I discharge

What bothers me what I despite

My life in fact I can't take

My temper is triggered

Fast spark in fire

when things do not go my way.

I Cry, cry, cry

I broke down cry

The heavens fell, the sky is black – the road is blocked

The God couldn't speak that time

I cry, I cry, I cry

Roads are closed

I couldn't see

With open eyes I could not see

My painful heart

I cry, cry, cry

I couldn't breathe … collapsed in pain

In despair

Why Goddess felt to see

I am here

help retrieve me back.

I cry, cry, cry

Where do I fail? Can you tell me?

Please speak aloud I can't hear

I collapsed ... fell

I cry, cry, cry

Loud he blasts... well, that is something you could control

It's up to you so we can all be well!

ANGER

Angry? That's so human!

The crooked bones in my chest, I feel pain

It reminds me of the past pain

Why don't I choose the weight of heaven instead?

We all know what anger does...

So, I'll be a better human to control my pride!

I choose how-to live-in fear or confidence,

The problem of being told, the problem with authority.

Choose to control my ego

And certainly, with generosity!

We never before counted such divides,

Couples, families, neighbors

Everyone from their side!

Life is short, my dear friend

So don't use anger, express love instead.

Today more than ever we need unity

Forget about anger in favor of harmony!

For ALL of you and me!

LOST

I got lost on my journey.

The eye longs, the heart longs

Fearing myself more than I could bear

With a cry of despair

I am hurt from the past

Bitter moments, hours, days

I suffered a defeat somewhere

Walking while crying while blind to see the light

at the end of the tunnel!

Now is the time for the brutal honesty hour.

I answer it

And,

I found ... the light at the end of the tunnel.

I don't quickly jump to conclusions about people

I don't feed memories that just keep going back. I asked,

What's quite possibly the most annoying thing that makes me mad?

What's my most persistent habit that gets me to resist?

I found purpose in life, fabulous triumph

To not give up on that… something…

Forgive and being forgiven will heal the wounds

I make it a goal that everyone wants.

That is the most important change that I should make

I answer these questions honestly, and act.

Now I see … it will be "the Great."

TROUBLES

Why do I have so many troubles, I asked
myself

Why do I keep on asking "why"?

Well, I lost my values, I lost myself

I lost my faith; I am in despair.

Like clouds in my thoughts

They are being pushed into my mind ...
more often than not.

I cannot forgive, it's so complex.

It's a barrier, I can't listen to my friends!

I broke down on the road again

Until someone came out who said:

If you could switch the gears

Rearrange your mind's files

It would not happen again.

as it shakes the "bad bug" that otherwise

 my mind can't.

I define, practice, with discipline, so I build

A life with no troubles, a life in bliss!

THE GIFT

Inside of me there is a place

where I can see so clearly

my "Why" so I can thrive.

I don't let my dreams slip away,

 my inner beauty,

I wrestle with my unseen villain

Who springs from the mind who is true?

to what's important, strangers too.

Stay motivated as I see,

life has up and down

twists and turns that I don't see!

 Face the fear and challenge, so I can grow.

I never forget to find my supportive shoulder

as we all need to lay on!

Thank you, God, for trusting me to share

all that among the gifts you care,

smiling, laughing with light,

loving through my open mind!

To discover the beauty that lies within

bring that up and feed it,

So, we all dream a new dream

Full of life!

NEVER GIVE UP!

I was a fool to think assess, compare, contrast,

above all, resistance to change!

It's a roller-coaster, my mind is screaming,

Why should I change, it's really unfulfilling!

Darkness takes me by the arm, made itself heard

the same old argument ... increasingly bitter... complicated.

Take down the love letters from the bookshelf,

the photographs, the desperate notes down to inhale!

Going like spiral cord, a self I could not conquer

Suddenly in the moonlight, it wakes up my insides!

I feel that I learned to assess my pain to discover

The change is part of a journey, delightful surprise.

I embrace the change and commit to it

to never give up the one I once believed!

All the beauty lies to what I discovered

to be resilient, stronger and brighter.

Gain clarity, courage and drive!

Bring up the beauty so we all can shine!

Dive deep to the insights and not to blame, complain.

I will never give up on love, compassion.

I will never give up believing in the beauty of human nature.

A LEADER!

One day a friend asked me:

What will be tomorrow? I am afraid!

I smiled and said:

There has been time that

my stomach rumbled from hunger.

Has been time that I caught cold

as my shoes were rotten, had holes.

Has been time that

my friend grabs my food to fight her hunger,

Has been time that rejection

was part of my every day,

But I never gave up the love and compassion,

I never gave up believing

in the goodness of human nature!

Has been time that people misjudged,

misinterpreted, and mistreated!

But I never gave up on loving and compassion

Has been time that

people's greed changed my way of life,

But I never gave up believing

the beauty within.

That is why you shouldn't be afraid

and never give up embracing

to be a great human civilization.

THE FUTURE GENERATION

Two worlds diverged on the road of life

But could the old and new journey together?

I wanted to be the traveler of the future,

stood and watched how the new took over

to take the lead. So be it!

 The burning feeling of exploring the new

Somewhere, ages and ages hence,

to build the foundation for the new generations

We judge, they judge how the new could be

So, we can build a great reality

We can build a great harmony

We can build a great community

We can build a great society!

Yes, we can,

Yes, we can when we think "WE" not "ME"

Yes, we can when the goodness prevails,

Yes, we can when we feed positivity.

Yes, we can when we demolish our greediness,

Yes, we can when we come together,

Yes, we can when we turn the ugliness into goodness,

Yes, we can when we embrace diversity.

Yes, we can when we have UNITY!

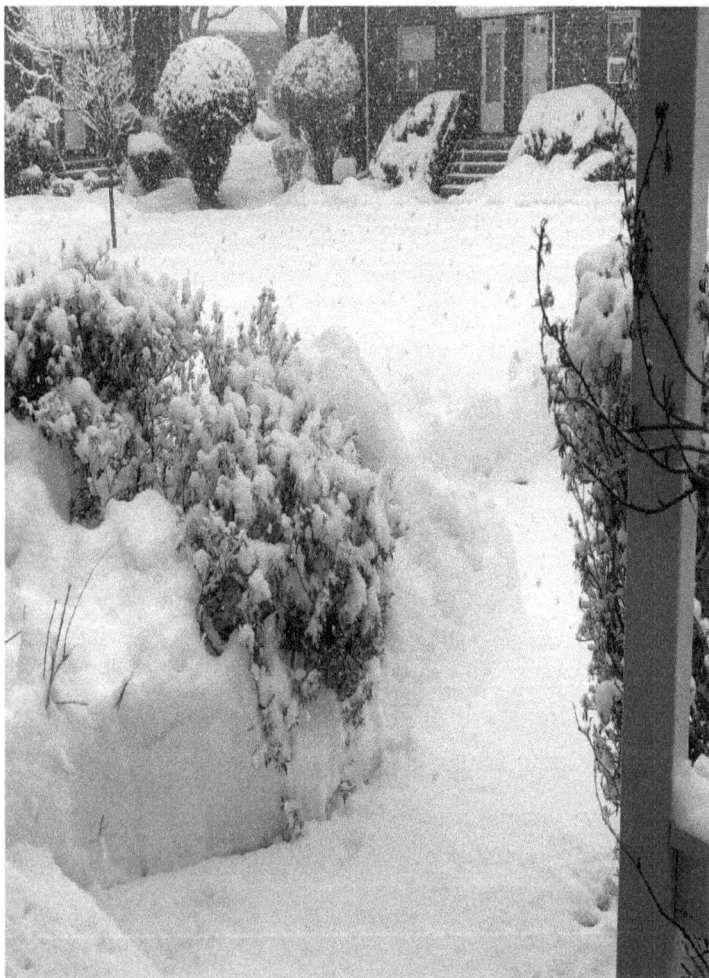

FIGHT!

Why do people fight, I asked myself one day!

I laugh with all my heart as it's so pitiful to say!

I cannot stand them when they try to teach me,

cannot ask others what they think of me

as I have a problem with authority!

What did I say and how I say it can break or make my life away!

Got to know my patterns ... they can bring resentment.

My ego, anger, fear of losing that battle.

I came up once and hollered! I came up twice and cried!

I stood there and I cried

my internal health crumbles,

my peace of mind gone when I lose my battle!

So, love to be loved and all hurt is gone!

AM I GRATEFUL?

The struggle is real, I bet it is

I forget what really matters

 what gratefulness is!

Get to work and complain about a coworker

complain about my boss

complain about the bus driver

 or the rain that took his time

 complain about my spouse,

complain about my children.

But I don't realize what really is given

salary, knowledge, care, skills,

above all great friendships.

I give my time, effort, care, enthusiasm, knowledge, experience.

I see a perfect harmony

everything ... our community, company, family, society,

I receive from all in multiple forms!

The is the basic law of life on giving and receiving

It's the Gratitude I feel

That is how happiness blossoms,

that is how the life is fulfilled!

The God created among humans

It is the duty of us to flourish and build

so, we pass it on, indeed!

OUR CHILDISH HEART!

We grow up and build our world!

We grow and be strong, we grow and be bold,

We grow and be trustworthy,

honest leaders and more…

But still in our inner cell resides

our childish heart that never dies!

We still remember our first ice cream,

our first teacher, our first dream.

Why for some reason do we forget to chase?

our inner child, the thirst for knowledge,

adventure, laugh and travel.

We count how many times we failed

But we don't count our blessings.

We are embarrassed

when someone get us off guard,

we cry when someone else leaves us,

we never say our hurtful truth

in fear of rejection, acceptance, dispute.

We often live someone else's dream.

Where is our inner child's curiosity, honesty?

To be fearless and never stop trying,

Go up and down the river of life

So, we can test how resilient we are

Promise ourselves to do something that we have never done,

Something that brings us back to life,

Something that brings back your childhood heart!

That is, my friend, the life that our inner child wants!

SPARK MY CURIOSITY

What would it be if I spark my curiosity?

Redefine my why, think in the way you do,

because it will be better for me and you!

How I got to this and how it will affect me,

as my tribe will suffer too!

Intervene my negativity with curiosity

Communicate my strengths, weakness,

mistakes too,

and if I am brave enough to know,

ask my tribe, as they know me too!

Recognize gaps, explore, invent, crave,
create.

I got the secret sauce to all satisfaction
that is there

From blossom to blossom, impossible
blossom.

BELIEVE

I am what I think I am,

believe what I think I am cut out for

put myself in a box, the small, little, scary box.

Never try to get out from it in fear of breaking down

stay forever in one place

watching others how they come out!

Believe me, it's scary too!

But wait!

What if, for a change, I believe I can do it too,

That is where I start believing yes, I can do it!

Write books, articles, create, teach too.

Oh, what a blessing, prosperity I feel when I am out of the little scary box too!

I am what I say I am!

Changed the conversation in my brain,

that is where the change, innovation, satisfaction and joy are.

That is when I believe I can do it!

I am what I think I am!

That's the miracle that we all can create!

HOPE

I meet a lady one day; her name is HOPE!

Oh what? – I said.

Where in the heaven did you find this name, that brings hope everywhere.

Hey, the hope we all so badly need!

Hope has been there when I have been scared

when the broken shadows my safety

when I cry, and I stumble from bed,

hope make me fearless of all I went through

hope is telling me *don't you fall I am here to hold you*

since I met the hope, my life has changed

and never been the same.

As my hope is everywhere there is a helping hand,

bring that hope that we all care!

Hope is the best friend for all, no matter where!

As the Hope is the one that helps us all

to carry on. So, we never feel alone.

It's the word that, when we say it, brings HOPE!

MY BOSS

Have you ever met a truly great boss?

I know one is hard to find, a pleasure to work with, Impossible to forget.

We build trust, loyalty, thrive in every difficulty,

build so everyone wins.

Care so everyone is nurtured.

Share so everyone cares,

Listen to everyone's needs so they can fix,

Learn and teach so we all grow indeed,

Impossible to forget and forever trust

That's my boss that built me up.

I certainly know that I am the fortunate one!

PART

II

WE CHOSE LOVE!

When we love, we always strive to become better than we are. When we strive to become better than we are, everything around us becomes better too.

– Paulo Coelho

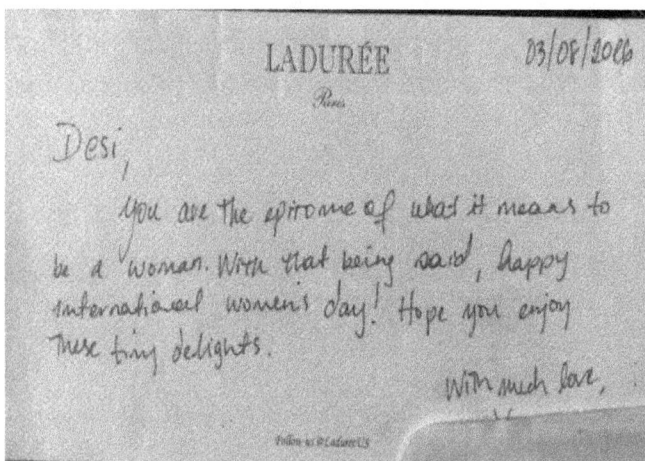

LADURÉE
Paris

03/08/2026

Desi,

You are the epitome of what it means to
be a woman. With that being said, happy
international women's day! Hope you enjoy
these tiny delights.

With much love,

Follow us @LaduréeUS

MY SOUVENIR

Oh, dear, how can I say

the beauty within of my souvenir,

holding it between my fingers

 the four flat pink roses

It's soap but it's not, it's a rose, but it's not!

It's purple, or red, it's white, or green

The person who sent me this wants me to know

That this world is better because of me

So, he asked, please be unapologetically me!

It's a kind of souvenir that never dies!

Has been with me for so many years

I will make sure to pass it on.

I will never, ever lose my precious souvenir.

He is lucky who comes across such a souvenir

As the beauty lay from the one that I received.

I come to say I wish you all

to find your souvenir and never let go!

WITHIN

Hey, I didn't realize you are a poet too

I didn't know either.

I know from childhood I love poems,

but I never even tried ... either!

There is place within us

that if we tap it, it will bring up

the beauty that resides in all of us!

Within us is everything

The good, the bad and ugly

Depends on what we choose

that will come up.

So, my dear friend, what is your choice?

Tap within to find that treasure that we all have

to share with us all.

It's our duty to find within

The beauty in everyone

So, we can share the love divine.

THE GIRL

She was a girl with a big dream

And love in her heart that anyone could see

She went up and down but never stopped

Chasing her dream from the inside out!

One can ask, how could she be real?

And the girl smiles as she knows what is real!

A BEAUTIFUL SOUL

Run, sing, laugh around a heavenly garden

Steering up tight receiving our Father's blessing

Sky is the limit of her precious dream

The music in her ear spills out unlimited venire

Walk in the classroom, hug everyone

Give and help from within

Enter at the office and greet everyone

Feel the needs and wants of everyone

Her lovely energy is contagious

As the adverse melts in her presence.

THE HERO WITHIN

We call Hero one that we adore

We call hero one that helps everyone

We call hero one that give his life for his country

But we don't call hero one that wins over oneself indeed!

BECOME WHAT?

For a moment I stopped and realized what I'd become

And saw every pinpoint of my life.

Fascinated with my life journey

Which I don't want to change a thing about.

Refocus on what part of *more of* I could repeat

And fulfilled over what I have become!

MY SON

My son, my mouth just blurts

My face shines, my heart sings

It's a feeling that rocks my world

It's that kind of feeling that only moms can feel!

He grows up, I go down

To flourish him with motherly care.

To fill the gaps

So, he can build the future that he cares about.

I feel his pain, I feel his laugh and look into his eyes

To find that sparkling joy

that he feels when he sees that I'm fine.

It's a bond that no one can break

No matter how many ups and downs.

As we both know what only we can know.

I thank you heaven for the given gift

It's priceless, it's precious, it's life in bliss

HEAVENS

Once she walks in the room

She brings music within her

The heavens give blessings

Calling me in silently with all her being.

It's such a relief to be with her!

She makes me feel mellow down to my soul!

She never complains, only a few can hold on!

The demand of family, work, community!

She is my inspiration, motivation, drive.

Thank you, heaven, thank God for me being recognized!

I know within her she has fire that never dies

It's contagious her smile that makes me realize

That life is short to waste for nothing

So, it's safe, I express my feelings, hopes, dreams.

To overtake my heart as she chooses so be it,

I still held her dear within and everything,

as certainly I know it's a life, it's bliss!

DREAM

The most wonderful of all things in life

is the discovery of another human being's dreams,

and helping them come true.

They turn to you for trust,

and you give it openly.

They look to you for inspiration, for answers

And you never let them down

You lift up their spirits and

take them in places they've never been.

You heal their troubles, the wounds too.

So many smiles depend on you!

You lift spirits, you bring smiles that never go away.

You brought us together so we can share!

When was the last time that you dreamed?

Spark that imagination, that little dream of you!

Flourish so we can enjoy too.

I know your dream, I see it too

In the way you look, in what you do

So let them all come true!

HEAVENLY FEELING

Dear Heaven, what was that night of unspoken love

A mix of fear, pride and passion

A volcano that couldn't wait to erupt!

I trembled inside and couldn't stop

my heart was rising, and you could hear it

come out of my chest in the infinite passion and idler!

He looked at me in disbelief and thrill

How can it be true that it could exist?

A soul that I could see through

Unstoppable passion, pride, and prejudice!

I looked at him in disbelief and thrill

How can it be true that it could exist?

A delightful soul that I could see through

And feel his love and cheer!

The world had stopped and everything around

To see two souls that

couldn't speak, but love!

Couldn't touch but feel!

Couldn't tell but show!

How heavenly love can be!

THE MAGIC

He stopped, I stopped

He looked, I looked

and tried to say something!

All night repeating, repeating, repeating what to say

At the end saying nothing!!!

Why on earth does one move?

To break that wall of fear

Imagine what heaven would be

Two souls blended in!

"O DIO Ti Prego"

What should I do!

Please help me

To jump into what we call infinity!

CONNECT THE DOTS

Connect the dots that's what I do

To find the hidden code of what love can
do!

The race is on, and I could clearly see the
hidden code

of how crazy love could be.

The power of love keeps me going

And try to connect the dots

To see how far I could go,

This crazy, crazy unspoken love!

SOLEMN LOVE

The solemn love surrounds my soul!

Indescribable feelings that only

in the dream one can dive on!

It's strange, it's brave, it's anguished, fearless

It's the heavens' creation.

It's a gift that the heavens gifted me,

I am rich to feel and believe in it!

The feelings, the infinite way

it fills the air with a heavenly breathless fun!

It's solemn moments that we are surround ourselves with

Those two crazy ones that keep going to forget that life is going on...

within the homes of the labyrinth of love.

It's a puzzle that no one else can find the

way out of,

 except from those two crazy ones!

In the solemn love that many are puzzled

Run, run, run

how could this happen?

Looks like it's unreal, looks like it's impossible

I promise it's real!

HE FILLS MY SOUL WITH SO MUCH LOVE

Walking through my life

Changes always come to my door

In big and small ways.

Some subtle and unnoticed

Some drastic and hard to handle!

But through my life's travels

Changing and rearranging

One thing that never changed

The beauty of your love

Commitment and delight.

You are such a strong, steady, sincere,

unpredictable one in the way you care, share and love!

You never cease to amaze me

with the constancy of your giving, your heart,

your time, the reason for my smile.

I thought it would be nice to let you know

that you have touched my heart,

my soul, with so much love,

and my special feeling for you will last forever.

You are the drive, the meaning of my life!

DIVINE

I don't know how God created Love

All I know is that it's a divine feeling that you gifted me!

On how you read me, how you help me,

How you look at me, how you adore me

How you heal my soul and my wounds!

How you build me up, how you deeply care!

Profoundly sensitive to my needs,

Unreasonably love you share.

So, can I ask you, God?

When you created Love

Why did you take out the logic?

WHERE DO I START!

To say how much I love you, how much I feel for you

No matter how far I am, I can feel your needs

I can feel your pain, I can feel your laugh

I can feel your dreams.

We went up and down so many times

And every time we come up

We are ready to jump into another dive.

It's meant to be a moment that no one can change

It's a journey that we chose to take.

The divine love that no one else can describe

How deep, how special our love is divine.

Our passion, our feelings, our Goddess inside!

A DAY TO REMEMBER!

It's late October on this beautiful day

I can't describe how content I am

It's divine harmony that everything felt in place

Like an impossible puzzle that finally reveals.

I feel the love all around me that everyone agrees

It's like a perfect orchestra that hardly waits

To perform the best performance, they can.

The divine harmony that the heavens have sent

For us to enjoy as much as we can.

IT'S GREAT TO BE ME!

I was born to learn how to be me!

I grew up a little and what do I see

An ocean of knowledge and wisdom to take in.

Where do I start? I asked my father.

He smiles and hugs me. "Look my daughter,

start where you are and love for who you are.

Ask inside you and you will find.

That will show you what you need and what you don't!"

I grew up more to see myself in the fire of life.

My mission and drive took me to the path

To serve and help with deep compassion and care!

My lifeline teaches me how to grow

To see what I didn't see.

I fell in Love with love itself,

to teach and show how great I already am.

Learn from everyone and still be me

For greatness I strive to live, give, serve and still be me!

I close my eyes and what I see is

a world of love that flourishes so the next generation can see.

Dear Friends, I want you to know greatness is up to me.

Strive to be better, unite my tribe, rebuild so we thrive.

Ignite my soul and never forget to still be ME!

I LOVE YOU!

I love you the troubled heart said,

All my life whom I ignored!

I love you the unbidden spirit said

Undeniably withhold

I love you the brilliant sun said

Waiting for me to shine

I love you the bright moon said

To dream with me tonight

I love you, beautiful nature, I said

with music that never dies

I love you my innocent son said

with patience, love

I love you my mom said

That so deeply love divine

I love you my sister said

That everything we shared

I love you my friend said

Sharing our laughs

I love you the neighbor said

Helping hand to hand

I love you All I just said

Blessed that I am alive

I love you, life I happily said

With music inside my heart

I love you God I heartily said

With faith that never dies

That is what matters in life I said

SIDEWALK CAFÉ

My friend asked me

What are your dreaming eyes dreaming?

Lost in my thoughts and smiling

I close my eyes so I can see a dream within me

walking at a Paris sidewalk café

you and me, holding our hands tenderly!

I am telling you everything by saying nothing...

Without speaking you give me the whole world!

It's my life-long dream that never faded.

Don't you settle down for less, you say

So, I jumped in and sank

on the images of our tender love

I hold deep in the hones of the labyrinth of my soul.

I never stopped believing in our pure tender love,

I close my eyes so I can see your beautiful eyes

smiling at me.

WHAT IS LOVE?

Love is looking at that special someone

The one that can make your world go around

And absolutely loving what you see

It is the nourishment for the soul.

It is a devotion constantly supporting our uncertainty!

It's a feeling deeper than the deepest

Sweeter than the sweetest

Gentler than the gentlest

It's a wonderful present so precious

you don't mess with it!

It's a dream that comes true!

It's your special miracle!

It's a new life, so live it!

You loved and you dreamed it!

A WONDERFUL THING!

How wonderful a thing is the spring?

Which comes as rejuvenation

Readjust, rearrange, reborn.

Carefully remove everything that does not belong,

Bad habits, toxicity, routines, old things

Oh, how refreshing, I am free!

Just like nature reborn from winter hibernation,

Flowers are blowing in the wind, it's heaven.

That's the time I reinvent everything I care about.

My actions are blessed from the universe too

While people carefully stare at me.

Positive movements, positive actions

That brings me closer and closer to the life that I love.

Spring is like perhaps the most beautiful thing

To let me know that I can do it again.

Fix any friction so I blossom

Just like flowers magically reborn

Rejuvenating without breaking

Repair, rebuild what is missing instead

That, my friend, is a blessing we all care about.

ABOUT THE AUTHOR

Desi Tahiraj—founder and CEO of <u>Desi Tahiraj Consulting, Inc.</u>, speaker, and author. Desi helps organizations in a holistic way by providing Human Resources/employee training, coaching, team building, mentoring, creating many online programs for burnout executives and those in a high-performance culture and much more; all these programs have been designed and based on her own experiences as an attorney and HR professional at Columbia University and corporations for over 17 years. On top of her busy schedule as an entrepreneur, Desi has been writing books called <u>Fail & Get & Never Give UP: The Power of Transformation</u>, which was published in October, 2020, and <u>Burnout – What's Next?: Solutions for High-Performer Burnout</u>, which was published in March 2021. She also has her fourth book coming in 2021 while being the speaker and running the <u>podcast</u> in hopes of helping executives, CEOs and staff to resolve their doubts/fears and enjoying the work/life balance since the pandemic started. Desi's works can also improve human performance in your business, motivate herself and others since the start of COVID, and advise all the aspiring women entrepreneurs out there.

Desi comes from communist Albania, an isolated and small country, where the communist regime killed and imprisoned twenty-seven members of her family for the single reason that they were not communists.

Her family was hit hard by that regime, where they were not allowed to love, marry, be educated or get jobs.

At a young age, she built deep compassion for people who suffered so much under communism including her own family. Later, she lost her first child; the second child was born with severe allergies to what is on 97% of the surface of the earth. Her ex-husband is a survivor of cancer and open-heart surgery, and Desi had become so sick that she had a near-death experience. During all these heartbreaking moments, she prayed to God to give her the courage and strength to help everyone in need. That is what motivated her to help her community and anyone who crosses her path.

As always, passion and enthusiasm for work and family came through. She looked up to learn from everyone while still being her unique self.

The roots of her leadership qualities came from her experience as a city attorney and from working with high achievers at Columbia University for 17 years. Later, she met her lifetime mentor, Mr. Jack Canfield, who pushed her beyond her limitations. All the outstanding qualities she assembled have been applied to her business as a high-performance coach for executives, a human resources consultant for universities and governmental agencies, and a burnout expert where she has created online programs. As an author, she created a podcast and became an international speaker. Nothing gives her more pleasure than transforming an organization and its executives. She created four online programs, wrote two books in six months, delivered over forty webinars in various subjects, wrote over twenty-six articles, and helped her community with volunteer work. She never stopped.

She is collaborating with the members of Fort Lee Chamber of Commerce, International Association of Women, International Association of Top Performers, Marquis Who's Who America, Columbia University Toastmasters, Train a Trainer Canfield Institute, Columbia University Alumni Association, IESE Business School Alumni Association and Bergen Volunteers New Jersey.

She loves to walk, hike, meditate, write, listen to classical music, go out in nature, spend time with her loved ones and travel when she has the chance.

"A ship in harbor is safe, but that is not what
ships are built for."
– John A. Shedd

LAST WORDS

I would like to thank you for reading my book and sharing it with others. I've enjoyed sharing it. As you probably realize, I have not been able to cover everything.

This book is about our journey of how to be a better human. It is about your trip, and I want to help you with it.

Validations and Takeaways: Have you identified your values and shared them with others? What types of power do your use and when?

Define success on your terms. Your purpose is like a north star, providing direction yet never reacting. It's what you stand for and it acts as a filter for proposing new opportunities. So, I have three amazing bonuses for you:

1. Text me at 201-951-1178, and I will send you one step a week on how to transform your life.
2. Type in the subject line "Our Human Race" and we will schedule for you a free, 40-minute consultation to help you discover how to thrive and be a high performer by turning around your burnout/failures and enhancing your life every day.
3. To find out how you can be part of my high achiever's mastermind group, please schedule a free call at the following link: https://desitahiraj.com/book-in-a-call/.

Thank You – Have a Fantastic Day, High Achievers!